MICHELANGELO

The Sistine Chapel

WINGS BOOKS

New York · Avenel, New Jersey

Published by Wings Books,
distributed by Outlet Book Company, Inc.,
a Random House Company,
40 Engelhard Avenue, Avenel, New Jersey, 07001.

Grateful acknowledgement is made to Art Resource and Superstock for permission to use their transparencies of the artwork.

Printed and bound in Singapore

Library of Congress Cataloging-in-Publication Data

Michelangelo Buonarroti, 1475–1564.
  Michelangelo : the Sistine Chapel.
    p.   cm.
ISBN 0-517-07764-7
    1. Michelangelo Buonarroti, 1475–1564—Catalogs.   2. Sistine Chapel (Vatican Palace, Vatican City)—Catalogs.   3. Miniature books—Catalogs.   I. Title.
ND623.B9A4   1992
759.5—dc20

92-988
CIP

8   7   6   5   4   3   2   1

...Try
To succour my dead pictures and my fame;
Since foul I fare and painting is my shame.

—MICHELANGELO

1. View of the entire chapel

2. The ceiling vault

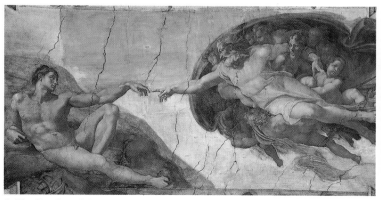

3. The Creation of Adam

4. The Creation of Adam, detail

5. The center ceiling: The Creations

6. The Creation of Eve

7. Adam and Eve Expelled from Eden

8. The Creation of the Sun and the Moon

9. The Creation of Adam, God Dividing the Land from the Water, and The Creation of the Sun and the Moon

10. The Sacrifice of Noah, The Expulsion from Eden, and The Creation
of Eve

11. The Drunkenness of Noah, The Deluge, and The Sacrifice of Noah

12. God Giving Order to Chaos, detail

13. The Delphic Sybil

14. The Delphic Sybil, detail

15. Bronze Nudes over the Persian Sybil

16. The Libyan Sybil

17. David and Goliath

18. Judith and Holofernes

19. The Ancestors of Christ

20. The Deluge

21. Ignudo and bronze medallion

22. Naason

23. The Prophet Jonah

24. The Last Judgment wall

25. Christ and the Virgin

26. Saint Bartholomew

27. The Damned

28. A damned soul

29. Saints Biagi, Catherine of Alexandria, and Sebastian

30. Angels and Archangels Calling the Reborn

31. The Blessed Ascending

Afterword

The most admired—and sought-after—artist of the sixteenth century, Michelangelo epitomized the Neo-Platonic ideal of divinely inspired genius. Although he believed the art of sculpture to be his true calling, his paintings in the Sistine Chapel in the Vatican in Rome are among the most celebrated works of his astonishing career.

Born in 1475, Michelangelo was apprenticed at age 13 to the painter Domenico Ghirlandaio in Florence. Less than a year later, he became part of Lorenzo Medici's "academy", the circle of writers and artists that dominated Florence during this period. After Lorenzo's death in 1492 and the ensuing fall of the Medici family, Michelangelo moved to Rome and undertook several commissions. In 1499 he completed his *Pieta*, a funerary monument for a French cardinal, which confirmed his reputation as a great artist:

> To this work let no sculptor, however rare a craftsman, ever think to be able to approach in design or in grace, or ever to be able with all the pains in the world to attain such delicacy and smoothness or to perforate the marble with such art as Michelangelo did therein...[1]

In 1501, Michelangelo returned to Florence where the new republican government commissioned him to sculpt the colossal *David*, the first full expression of Michelangelo's heroic style:

Nor has there ever been seen a pose so easy, or any grace to equal that in this work, or feet, hands and head so well in accord, one member with another, in harmony, design, and excellence of artistry.[2]

Pope Julius II summoned Michelangelo to Rome once again in 1505 to construct a mausoleum, a project that would haunt Michelangelo for the next forty years. His magnificent statue of Moses, and the incomplete *Struggling Slave* and *Dying Slave*, are all that remain of the unfinished endeavor.

In 1508, when the pope requested that Michelangelo abandon his work on the tomb to paint the ceiling of the Sistine Chapel, the artist angrily protested that he was a sculptor, not a painter. Michelangelo suspected that his rivals arranged the commission:

In this manner it seemed possible to Bramante and other rivals of Michelangelo to draw him away from sculpture, in which they saw him to be perfect, and to plunge him into despair, they thinking that if they compelled him to paint, he would do work less worthy of praise, since he had no experience of colors in fresco.[3]

But Michelangelo could not defy the authority of the pope. On a scaffolding of his own design, where he lay on his back 87 feet above the floor, Michelangelo undertook the most heroic feat in the history of art. Over a period of four years, displeased with the work of the assistants he had brought from Florence, he worked alone to create the momentous masterpiece.

Built by Pope Sixtus IV in 1473, the Sistine Chapel was meant, of course, to be a place of worship; but it was also considered a monument to the power of the Catholic Church. The walls were graced with frescoes of scenes from the Old and New Testaments executed by Perugio, Signorelli, Botticelli and others during the 1480s.

The ceiling itself is a vast area—133 feet by 43 feet; its decoration was Michelangelo's first major fresco. Initially, Michelangelo, impatient to continue work on Julius's tomb, planned to paint the Apostles in the lunettes and to cover the ceiling itself with conventional decorations. But, as Michelangelo wrote:

> Having begun work, it seemed to me that it would turn out poorly....[The Pope] then gave me a new contract so that I could make it as I wanted and [do] what would satisfy me...[4]

The architectural structure of the ceiling, a shallow, barrel-shaped vault flanked by concave triangles, served as Michelangelo's starting point. Whereas a painter might have treated the ceiling as a flat surface, Michelangelo had the expertise of a sculptor, used to working with three-dimensional surfaces.

> Michelangelo accepted the curved surface of the ceiling as it offered itself, and in it evoked an architectonic framework and a world of gigantic figures which personify the vital energies potentially present in the ceiling itself.[5]

Along the curving surface, he painted simulated arches that extend from the actual pilaster along the walls of the chapel. However, within each frame Michelangelo let the powers of his imagination and his sense of the aesthetic rule. The impression is at once one of dramatic excitement and serene tranquility. As a whole, the ceiling frescoes follow no rules of perspective, thus demand no fixed point of view. Each scene is defined by the figure within it; every figure is granted its own integrity. All display Michelangelo's mastery in drawing the human figure, his knowledge of human anatomy, and his belief that painting should mimic as nearly as possible the rounded, three-dimensional forms achieved in sculpture.

Michelangelo set out to tell a story that would portray both the humanist and religious traditions of Renaissance Italy. Its focus was the evolution of man's spiritual growth, with the advent of Christianity as the final culmination. From pagan tradition, the Five Sibyls (plates 13, 14, and 16), holding books and scrolls believed to contain prophetic passages of the coming of Christ, represent man's earliest beliefs in divinely inspired messengers. The Hebrew Prophets express the intimate connection between the Old and New Testament. These philosophers and thinkers who recognized God's revealed truths were forerunners to the Christians.

The symbolic significance of certain figures remains somewhat of a mystery. Scattered throughout the fresco, the *ignudi* (plates 15 and 21) have been considered spiritual beings positioned somewhere between humankind and divinity and interpreted as embodiments of the Platonic ideal of love that sets the soul free from the body. Finally, within triangles and lunettes, Michelangelo painted ordinary mortals, static figures unilluminated by the light of revelation (plate 22).

The paintings within the central strip of the vaulted ceiling—four large panels portraying the *Creation of the Sun and Moon* (plate 8), the *Creation of Adam* (plates 3 and 4), *Adam and Eve Expelled from Eden* (plate 7) and the *Deluge* (plate 20) and five smaller panels devoted to other images from *Genesis*—truly awe the viewer. Michelangelo actually began with the *Deluge*; as he moved backwards in history towards the creation, the figures become bigger, the composition more sculptural—a striking record of the development of his technique and understanding of fresco as his work continued. Michelangelo's grandest figure exemplifies the evolution of his work:

> The Creator is not only a gigantic man endowed with insuperable prowess. Through the energy of the plastic and dynamic structure of God's figure, the Creator is also conceived as the primeval force of nature: he seems really to incarnate the irresistible, primeval force of the cosmos.[6]

Each scene of God's creation of the world reflects an aspect of the artist's creative process, moving from the control of chaos in *God Giving Order to Chaos* (plate 12) to the infusion of energy in *Creation of the Sun and Moon* to the refining of details in the *Separation of Water from Land*. The *Creation of Adam*, with God's hand outstretched, is an unsurpassed image of the mystery of creation, the passing of the "divine spark" that animates matter. It is, as Vasari wrote:

> A figure of such a kind in its beauty, in the attitude, and in the outlines that it appears as if newly fashioned by the first and supreme Creator rather than by the brush and design of mortal man.[7]

The *Creation of Eve* (plate 6) marks the transition from Michelangelo's exploration of creation to that of humankind's fall into sin and suffering. The *Deluge* and *The Sacrifice of Noah* (plate 11) powerfully portray the consequence of sin; the *Drunkenness of Noah* (plate 11) presents a dismal vision of man's ultimate degradation.

Almost a quarter of a century after he completed the ceiling, Michelangelo was summoned by Pope Paul III to paint *The Last*

Judgment (plate 24) on the altar wall. Now 61, Michelangelo once again mounted a scaffolding in the Sistine Chapel. The fresco bears witness not only to the changes in the world's fortunes—the Reformation was shaking the political and religious foundations of Europe—but to Michelangelo's own despair. "I live in sin, I live dying within myself," he wrote.[8] In *The Last Judgment,* Michelangelo brought to life the hell-fire sermons he had heard in his youth and the dramatic terror of Dante's *Inferno* which he had studied closely.

The majestic Christ as the center of the work (plate 25) is surrounded by the souls of the dead, both blessed (plate 31) and damned (plate 27), rising and falling, escorted by angels and demons. The figure of St. Bartholomew (plate 26) reveals the extent of Michelangelo's despair: the face on the flayed skin the saint holds in his hand is that of Michelangelo himself. It is a grim, and moving, self-portrait.

Though Vasari and others recognized *The Last Judgment* as a true masterpiece,[9] many people were outraged by it, as one person angrily wrote to Michelangelo:

> I as one baptized, am ashamed of the license, so harmful to the spirit, which you have adopted....Is it possible that you, who as a divine being do not condescend to the society of men, should have done such a thing in the foremost temple of God?[10]

The uproar reached such proportions that later in the century Pope Pius IV had the artist Daniele da Volterra paint clothing on many of the nude figures.

Toward the end of his life, turning more and more to the fervent Catholicism of the Counter-Reformation, Michelangelo wrote in a poem:

Now I know well how that fond phantasy,
    Which made my soul the worshipper and thrall of earthly art is
        vain...
Painting nor sculpture now can lull to rest
    My Soul, that turns to His great love on high...[11]

Today many people contemplate Michelangelo's great statues, from the *David* of his youth to his final Rondanini *Pieta*. Many continue to marvel at the sublimity of St. Peter's Basilica, which he designed when he was seventy years old. However, art lovers and artists alike, many of whom still look to the chapel ceiling as the apex of great painting, would certainly agree with Vasari's words about the Sistine Chapel:

> This work, in truth, has been and still is the lamp of our art, and has bestowed such benefits and shed so much light on the art of painting, that it has served to illuminate a world that has lain in darkness for so many hundreds of years.[12]

This praise remains true more than four centuries later.

NOTES

1. Giorgio Vasari, *The Great Masters* (New York: Park Lane), 224
2. Ibid, 227
3. Ibid, 239
4. *The Complete Works of Michelangelo* (New York: Reynal and Company), 200
5. *Treasures of the Vatican* (New York: Portland House), 109
6. *The Complete Works of Michelangelo*, 216
7. *The Great Masters*, 242
8. *The Renaissance* (Washington, D.C.: National Geographic Society), 168
9. *The Great Masters*, 273
10. Letter from Aretino to Michelangelo, 1545, quoted in Andre Chastel, *Art of the Italian Renaissance* (New York: Arch Cape Press), 190-91
11. Will Durant, *The Renaissance* (New York: Simon and Schuster), 717
12. *The Great Masters*, 241